Pat Moon
Illustrated by Lisa Smith

One day, Tina and Rita found a dog.
The dog was sitting at their door.

"Shoo!" said Mum.

But the dog did not shoo.
She ran into their house.

"Can we keep her?" said Tina.

"No," said Mum. "She has her own family. Look at her tag. Her name is Scruff!"

There was a phone number on the tag. Mum phoned, but no one answered. So she left a message.

Just then, their cat Ginger meowed. Scruff was eating Ginger's dinner!

"Bad dog!" said Rita.

“Scruff wants some food,” said Tina.
Mum gave her some food.

“There you go,” Mum said.

Ginger looked cross.

Then Scruff got into Ginger's bed!
"Meow!" cried Ginger.
"Bad dog!" said Mum. "That is Ginger's bed."

Later, Dad came home. He looked at Scruff.
“Who is this?” he asked.
“It’s Scruff!” said Rita.
“I can see that,” said Dad.

At dinner, Dad's food went missing.

"Where has my food gone?" he asked.

Scruff was eating it!

"Bad dog!" said Tina.

No one phoned back about Scruff. Tina was happy, but Mum was not. She put a notice in the newspaper.

FOUND

LITTLE DOG NAMED SCRUFF.

Please call 559876.

"If no one phones about Scruff, can we keep her?" Tina asked Mum.

"No," said Mum. "If no one phones, we will take her to the animal shelter."

The next day, Scruff was very bad. She took Dad's shoe.

Later, a chicken went missing.
"Where can it be?" asked Mum.
Scruff and Ginger were missing too.

The family went to look for Scruff and Ginger. They were in the garden. They had eaten the chicken!

“Bad dog!” said Dad.
“Bad Ginger!” said Mum.
“Look!” Tina said. “Ginger likes Scruff now!”

The next day, Mum found a hole in the garden. Dad looked in the hole.

"What is that?" he asked.

"It's your shoe!" said Tina.

"Bad dog!" said Mum and Dad.

"Oh, Scruff," said Tina. "Please be good so we can keep you."

The next day, Scruff tried to be good. She chased a cat from the garden. But Mum was cross.

"Bad dog!" she cried.

Scruff looked sad.

"Just don't do it again, Scruff," said Mum. She gave Scruff a little pat.

When Dad got home, Scruff jumped on him.

"Get down, Scruff!" Dad cried. "I'm all scruffy now!"

So Scruff licked Dad. She wanted to lick him clean. Tina and Rita laughed. Mum and Dad laughed too.

“They like you now, Scruff,” Tina told her. I’m going to ask *again* if I can keep you.” Tina went to see Mum and Dad. But they had bad news…

“Scruff’s family phoned,” Mum said. “They want to take her home.”

Mum and Dad looked sad. Rita cried. Tina cried and cried and cried.

The next day, Scruff's family took her home.
"I'm going to miss Scruff," said Mum.
"Me too," said Rita.
"Meow," Ginger said.

Dad was reading the newspaper.

"The animal shelter has lots of dogs that need good homes," he said.

"But, I want Scruff back!" said Tina.

"Let's just go and see," said Dad.

The family went to the animal shelter. They looked at the dogs.

The first dog looked like a good dog. She was eating her dinner. The next dog was a clean dog. He was sitting down. The last dog was a scruffy dog. He was running around, chasing his tail.

"We want that dog!" cried Tina and Rita and Mum and Dad.